# How Tiger and Lion Became Friends

## WRITTEN BY: ZAIRE MARTIN
## ILLUSTRATED BY: MARCELLOUS LOVELACE

First American Paperback Edition 2014
Text copyright © 2012 Zaire Martin
Illustrations copyright © 2012 Marcellous Lovelace
All rights reserved. Published in the United States by KHOPIA LLC.
www.khopia.com
ISBN 9780692219508

Tiger and Lion were not good friends.

They would always fight.

Every morning they said Good Morning to Bull, Goose, Kangaroo, Cat, Tarantula and Dog.

But Lion didn't say Good Morning to Tiger, and Tiger didn't say Good Morning to Lion either.

When it was time to eat, Tiger put food in his mouth.

He thought it was meat, but actually Lion switched his meat with vegetables.

Lion laughed and ran.

Tiger was so mad, that his face turned red.

He was not happy about this.

Then it was time to play in the waterhole.

Since Tiger and Lion are both cats, they both hate swimming in the water.

Tiger pushed Lion in the water.

Lion was so mad, that his face turned red.

He was not happy about this.

The other animals were very annoyed by Lion and Tiger.

"What is wrong with them," Goose said.

"Stop, we're through with you guys," said Bull.

"If you want to be our friends, you two have to be friends first."

"Do you want to be friends?" Lion asked Tiger.

"Whatever, " said Tiger. "I just want to be friends with them."

Lion then said to Tiger,
"You know, we both have a lot in common."

Tiger says, "What do you mean?"

So Lion and Tiger talk all night on top of the trees and laugh about how much they really have in common.

The next morning, they are so sleepy that they don't even tell the other animals that they are now friends.

At breakfast Lion yawns, "Good Morning Bull, Goose, Kangaroo, Cat, Tarantula and Dog."

Then he turns to his new friend Tiger and says, "Good Morning Tiger."

Tiger replies with a smile, "Good Morning to you too."

All the other animals are surprised but they are very happy that Lion and Tiger are now Friends.

They learn that even those who are not friends can become new friends.

The End.

## About the Author

My name is Zaire Martin. I was born and raised in Chicago, Illinois. I am 7 years old. There are five people in my family. One of my favorite subjects is science. I also have a dog. He is a golden labrador retriever. He is really big and loves treats. He tried to bite me once, but he has never bit me.

I would like to thank Marcellous, my dad's friend, for drawing my pictures. I dedicate this book to a very special person who taught me about folk tales.

www.ingramcontent.com/pod-product-compliance
Lightning Source LLC
Chambersburg PA
CBHW041240040426
42445CB00004B/103